Usborne

my very first Space book

Illustrated by Lee Cosgrove
Written by Emily Bone
Designed by Alice Reese

The night sky

When the Sun sets, the sky grows dark. You'll start to see twinkling stars. What you're looking at is just a tiny part of SPACE.

Space is so enormous, no one knows how big it really is.

Someone who studies space is called an astronomer.

The Moon is the brightest thing in the night sky.

This is a space agency, where people design spacecraft and train to go into space.

Rocket ready to launch

People who fly into space are called astronauts.

What is space?

We live on planet Earth. Space is everything around our planet. There are lots of incredible things out there.

Stars

Moons

Planets

Galaxies

Space probe

TV satellites
send pictures to
your television.

Space rocks,
called asteroids

Rocket blasting
into space

Comet

Earth is covered by a layer of gases, called the atmosphere.

This is planet Earth.
From space, it looks like
a green, blue and white ball.

The blue areas
are water.

The green parts
are land.

The Moon

The Moon is a big ball of rock
that travels around the Earth.

The lighter areas
are the tops of
high mountains.

There's no air or
water, and nothing
lives on the Moon.

The dark patches
are huge holes,
called craters.

The first astronauts on the Moon left a flag to show they had visited.

Lunar module

Filming

Collecting Moon rocks

Space suit

Moon buggy

Space school

Before astronauts go into space,
they have to do a lot of training.

Learning everything about
space and space travel

Getting very fit and
being tested on it

Finding out how to work
spacecraft controls

Emergency
escape drills

Learning what to do if
they crash into the sea

Using tools

Learning the languages of
astronauts from different countries

Repairing a pretend spacecraft
while floating in a huge water tank

Talking to experienced
astronauts

Being given a mission and
meeting the rest of the crew

Lift-off!

A rocket, called a launch vehicle, flies
a team of three astronauts into space.

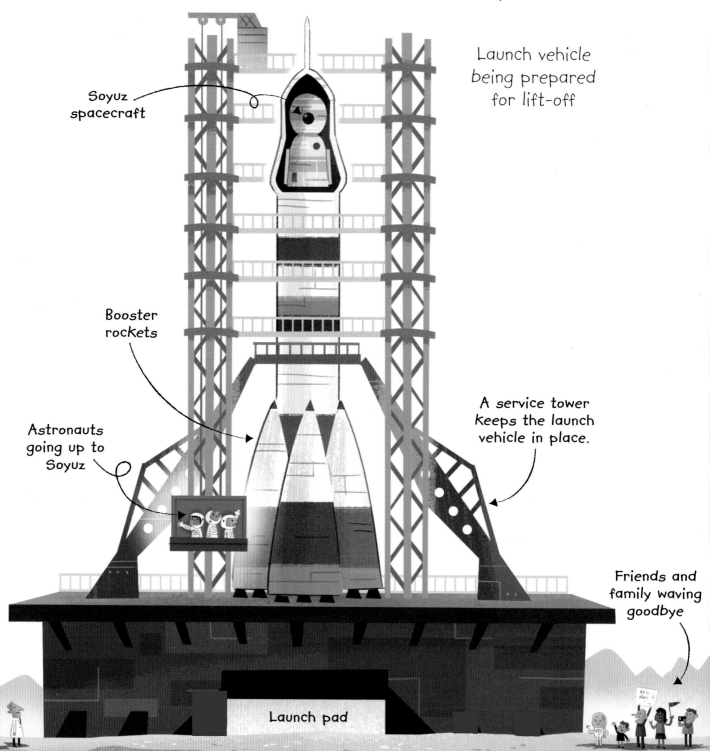

Soyuz
spacecraft

Launch vehicle
being prepared
for lift-off

Booster
rockets

A service tower
keeps the launch
vehicle in place.

Astronauts
going up to
Soyuz

Friends and
family waving
goodbye

Launch pad

Astronauts inside Soyuz
getting ready for lift-off

Booster rockets firing

LIFT-OFF!

Booster rockets falling
back to Earth

Launch vehicle falling back
and Soyuz flying away

Space station

In space, astronauts live and work in a spacecraft called the International Space Station. It flies high above the Earth.

Soyuz joins up with the Space Station and astronauts go in.

Storage room

Astronauts relaxing

Robot arm for moving equipment

Living in space

On the Space Station, everything floats.
This is what happens during a day:

Washing using
dry shampoo

Using the toilet

Exercising for two hours

Most food
comes in
packets.

Eating

Repairing the outside of
the Space Station

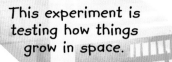

This experiment is testing how things grow in space.

Doing experiments

Relaxing

Dirt could get into equipment and break it.

Cleaning

An astronaut guides the spacecraft up to the Station.

Receiving deliveries from supply spacecraft

Unpacking supplies

Talking to family back home

Taking photos of Earth

Sleeping bags are strapped to the wall.

Going to sleep

Spacewalk

There's no air in space. When astronauts go on a spacewalk outside the Space Station, they have to wear a space suit that gives them air and keeps them safe.

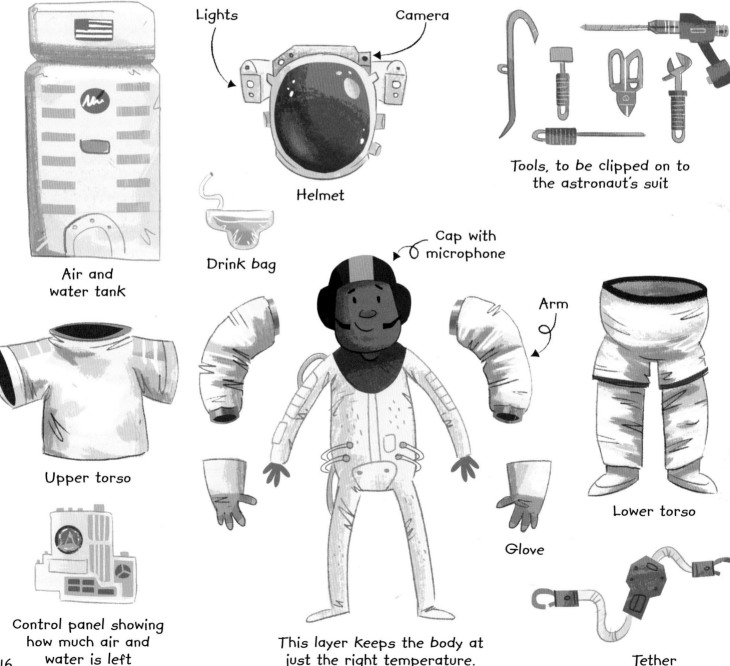

Air and water tank

Lights

Camera

Helmet

Drink bag

Tools, to be clipped on to the astronaut's suit

Cap with microphone

Arm

Upper torso

Glove

Lower torso

Control panel showing how much air and water is left

This layer keeps the body at just the right temperature.

Tether

Astronauts go on spacewalks in pairs.

Checking spacesuits
and putting them on

Going into an airlock
for 24 hours

Opening the exit hatch

Attaching the tether and going outside

Receiving instructions from Earth

Fitting new equipment
to the Space Station

Drinking from
the drink bag

Returning to the
Space Station

The Solar System

The Earth is one of eight planets that travel around the Sun. The Sun and the planets are known as the Solar System.

Mercury

Earth

This is the Moon. Other planets have moons, too.

The Sun

Sometimes, space rocks crash into planets.

Venus

Venus is covered in thick, poisonous clouds.

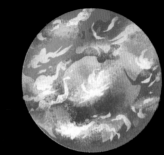

Mars

Jupiter

Neptune

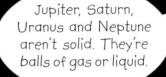

Jupiter, Saturn, Uranus and Neptune aren't solid. They're balls of gas or liquid.

The Great Red Spot is a huge storm.

Jupiter is the biggest planet. It has more than 60 moons.

A comet is a ball of gas, ice and dust.

Uranus

It leaves a bright tail behind it.

Uranus has rings made from ice and dust.

The Asteroid Belt is a big group of space rocks.

This is Pluto. It's a dwarf planet.

Saturn

Saturn's rings are made from chunks of rock and ice.

Exploring Mars

Small spacecraft have flown vehicles, called rovers, to Mars. Rovers find out more about the rocks and air on Mars.

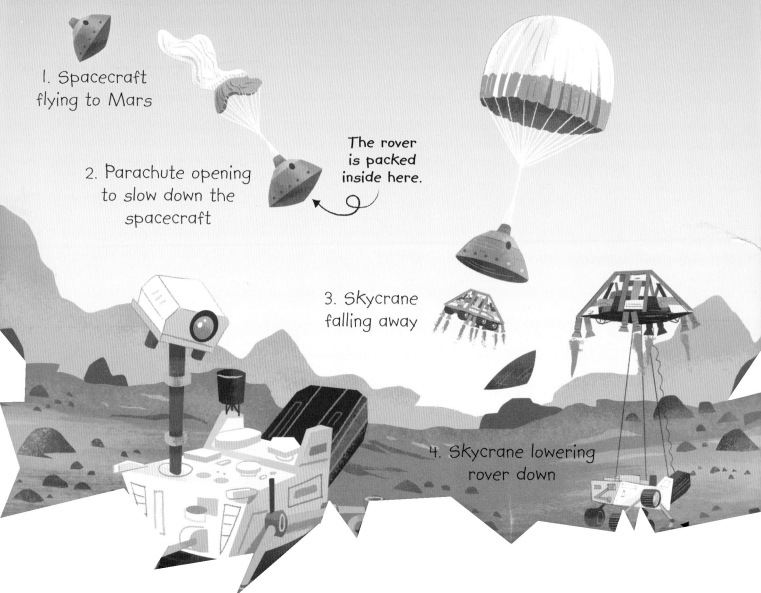

1. Spacecraft flying to Mars

2. Parachute opening to slow down the spacecraft

The rover is packed inside here.

3. Skycrane falling away

4. Skycrane lowering rover down

Receiving instructions
from Earth

Exploring different places
and taking pictures

Firing a laser and drilling into rocks
to find out what's inside them

Scooping up dust
and testing it

Finding out about the
weather on Mars

Sending pictures
back to Earth

Stars

Stars are massive balls of very, very hot gases.
The Sun is a star. This is what it looks like close up.

Gases bubbling on
the Sun's surface

This is a solar
flare, a big
explosion.

From Earth, the Sun
looks bigger than
other stars because
it's our closest star.

There are different types of stars.

Our Sun is a type
of star called a
yellow dwarf.

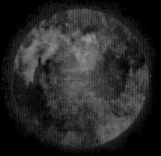

The least powerful
stars are called
red dwarfs.

The biggest and most
powerful stars are
called supergiants.

Life of a star

A new star is formed out of a huge, swirling cloud of gas and dust called a nebula.

This is the
Tarantula Nebula.

1. Part of the nebula gets thicker and hotter.

2. Slowly, it turns into a hot ball.

3. This becomes a new star.

Stars glow and burn for millions and millions of years. Then, they start to change.

Different stars change in different ways.

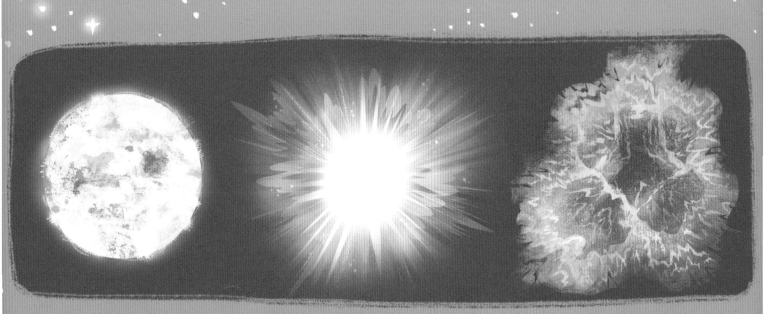

1. A yellow dwarf star gets cooler, bigger and duller.

2. Its outer layers puff away.

3. Eventually, a white dwarf star is left behind.

1. A supergiant star gets bigger and brighter.

2. It explodes. This is called a supernova.

3. A big cloud of gas is left behind.

Great galaxies

Millions and millions of stars form massive groups, called galaxies. Galaxies come in different shapes and sizes.

This is a spiral galaxy.

This is called the Cartwheel Galaxy, because it looks like a wheel.

Some galaxies look like bright balls.

Other galaxies are slowly joining together.

The Sun is just one star in a spiral galaxy called the Milky Way.

Lots of stars are being formed in this bright bulge.

The Sun is somewhere around here.

Looking at space

Telescopes help people to see things in space that are very far away. There are lots of different types.

Space telescopes take pictures of things in space.

Hubble Space Telescope

Probes fly around planets.

Optical telescope

Radio telescopes look for faraway stars and galaxies.

Mirrors make things look bigger.

With telescopes or binoculars you can see things in more detail.

Hubble is a famous space telescope.

A spacecraft taking Hubble into space

Hubble flying around the Earth

Astronauts have been sent to make repairs.

Astronauts fitting new cameras onto Hubble

Radio dishes on Earth collect the pictures, then send them to computers.

Hubble taking lots of pictures and sending them back to Earth

Each swirl and dot in this picture is a faraway galaxy.

Scientists studying the pictures

Stargazing

Even without using a telescope, you can see lots of things in the night sky.

Stars can *be joined up* to make pictures, called constellations.

Sirius is the brightest star in the sky.

The Great Dog

Orion the Hunter

The Big Dipper or the Plough

The Southern Cross

The International
Space Station passing
overhead looks like a
bright star.

The planet
Jupiter

This is the brightest
part of the Milky
Way galaxy.

The Moon

A shooting star

Sometimes, glowing lights appear.
This is called an aurora.

The planet
Venus

What you can see in the sky changes
depending on the time of year and where
you are in the world. To find out more
about constellations and space in general,
go to the Usborne Quicklinks website,
www.usborne.com/quicklinks and type
in the name of this book.

Index

A
asteroids, 5, 18, 19
Asteroid belt, 19
astronauts, 3, 7, 8-9,
    10, 11, 12, 13, 14, 15,
    16, 17, 29
astronomers, 2
atmosphere, 5
aurora, 31

B
Big Dipper, 30
binoculars, 28

C
comets, 5, 19
constellations, 30-31

E
Earth, 4, 5, 6, 13, 15,
    17, 18, 29

G
galaxies, 4, 26-27,
    28, 29
Great Dog, 30

H
Hubble Space
    Telescope, 28, 29

I
International Space
    Station, 12-17, 31

J
Jupiter, 19, 31

L
lunar module, 7

M
Mars, 18, 20-21
Mercury, 18
Milky Way, 27, 31

Moon, 3, 6-7, 18, 31
moons, 4, 18, 19

N
nebula, 24
Neptune, 19

O
Orion the Hunter, 30

P
planets, 4, 18, 19,
    28, 31
Pluto, 19

R
rockets, 3, 5, 10-11
rovers, 20-21

S
satellites, 5
Saturn, 19
shooting stars, 31

Solar System, 18-19
Southern Cross, 30
Soyuz, 10, 11, 12
space agency, 3
spacecraft, 3, 8, 9,
    10, 11, 12-13, 15,
    20, 29
space probes, 5, 28
spacesuits, 7, 16, 17
spacewalks, 13, 16-17
stars, 2, 4, 22-25, 26,
    27, 28, 30, 31
Sun, 2, 18, 22, 23, 27
supernova, 25

T
telescopes, 2, 28-29

U
Uranus, 19

V
Venus, 18, 31

Photographic manipulation by Nick Wakeford and John Russell
Series Editor: Ruth Brocklehurst   Series Designer: Josephine Thompson

Photo credits
The publishers are grateful to the following for permission to reproduce material:
The Moon © Stockbyte/Getty Images (the Moon); Stars © SOHO/ESA/NASA/Science Photo Library (the Sun); Life of a star © NASA, ESA,
and the Hubble Heritage Team (STScI/AURA) (the Tarantula Nebula); Looking at space © NASA, ESA, G. Illingworth, D. Magee, and
P. Oesch (University of California, Santa Cruz), R. Bouwens (Leiden University), and the HUDF09 Team (Hubble 'deep field' group of galaxies).
Every effort has been made to trace and acknowledge ownership of copyright.
If any rights have been omitted, the publishers offer to rectify this in any subsequent editions following notification.